jealousy
last straw strategies

last straw strategies
99 tips to bring you back from the end of your rope

jealousy

Michelle Kennedy

BARRON'S

First edition for the United States, its territories
and possessions, and Canada published in 2004 by
BARRON'S EDUCATIONAL SERIES, INC.
by arrangement with
THE IVY PRESS LIMITED

All inquiries should be addressed to:
Barron's Educational Series, Inc.,
250 Wireless Boulevard
Hauppauge, New York 11788
www.barronseduc.com

International Standard Book Number
0-7641-2720-9

Library of Congress Catalog Card No.
2003107435

Every effort has been taken to ensure that all
information in this book is correct. This book is not
intended to replace consultation with your doctor,
surgeon, or other healthcare professional. The author
and publisher disclaim any loss, injury, or damage
incurred as a consequence, directly or indirectly, of
the use and application of the contents of this book.

This book was conceived,
designed, and produced by
THE IVY PRESS LIMITED
The Old Candlemakers
West Street, Lewes
East Sussex BN7 2NZ

Creative Director PETER BRIDGEWATER
Publisher SOPHIE COLLINS
Editorial Director STEVE LUCK
Design Manager TONY SEDDON
Senior Project Editor REBECCA SARACENO
Designer JANE LANAWAY
Illustrator EMMA BROWNJOHN

Printed in China
9 8 7 6 5 4 3 2 1

contents

jealousy
introduction

The sight of your sweet-faced toddler in a jealous rage is guaranteed to send a shiver down the parental spine—all that fury with nowhere to go. One of the reasons that most of us find it so disturbing is because the emotion is uncomfortably close to what we experience ourselves, only we adults keep the green-eyed monster locked away inside.

When you are trying to deal with jealousy-fueled bad behavior, you need to put yourself in your little monster's shoes, because if you understand why they feel bad, you can help them out of their black hole. The other thing to remember is timing and development: for the first two years your child is "egocentric," that is, the center of their own world, and is unable to understand the concept of sharing and the feelings of others. For example, the child will "hang on" to toys and howl with rage if you try to give these to another child or another child tries to grab them.

As your child grows, you can help them to understand concepts such as sharing, and that daddy gets to cuddle mom, and vice versa, every now and then. By focussing on the situation, using imagination, sympathy, and a good helping of reassurance, you can clear the storm clouds away and restore calm to your loving child remarkably quickly. Jealousy can be tough and is sometimes disguised, so here are 99 strategies that have been proven to work in the majority of situations.

the new
baby

Despite the growing evidence to the contrary—mom's big belly, a new crib in the house, new toys, and smaller diapers—your child will not fully grasp the idea of a new baby until they actually come through the door. And they usually do arrive, much to your child's dismay, in mom's arms. "What is this squirming, loud, sometimes smelly thing that my parents have decided will live in my house—maybe even my room?" a toddler must think. This confusion can make a child alternately very angry and very protective. There are ways, however, to prevent a huge amount of jealousy, although the older child will always, always be at least a little jealous of the younger ones (and vice versa, eventually). After all, I'm the oldest of three and I still get jealous sometimes!

encourage dad

Even if dad is the kind of dad who does fun outings on the weekends, but leaves the daily, well, let's face it, drudgery, to mom, get him to pitch in and enlist the older child as his able assistant. My husband and the kids helped with chores while I nursed the baby—the chores got done and they could talk about all sorts of things (why the sky is blue, how to get chocolate cake for dinner...). Their bond will be important when the new baby arrives.

the new baby

during pregnancy

If possible, while you're pregnant, take your toddler to hospital appointments with you so that he can see his sibling on the scan and hear the heartbeat on the Doppler. You could also show him the picture of his own scan and explain what it felt like to have him in your tummy. Many hospitals have "older brother and sister" programs in which the child can tour the hospital, take a baby care class, and make presents for the baby.

aggression

If your toddler is extremely jealous of the new baby—
perhaps even violently so—then you have a bigger problem
on your hands. If your toddler bites or otherwise harms the
baby, you need to act quickly. First, immediately remove
your toddler from the baby. Place him in your "time out"
spot and let him know, without yelling or smacking, that
you will not allow him to harm the new baby. You might
find that the toddler was not being vengeful, but just
reacting to the baby grabbing a fistful of hair (a common
new baby action). Hold a little class on the "only way we
touch the baby." For the next few weeks, make sure your
toddler is never alone with the baby, but don't be obvious
about it. Bear in mind that your child could be looking for
attention and might need some more one-on-one time. If
further "attacks" occur, consult a professional.

the new baby

the first visit

On his first visit to the hospital (check out the hospital rules beforehand), make a fuss of your firstborn when you see him, then show him his new baby brother or sister. Again, talk about "your baby sister" rather than "the new baby." Let him do as much as he feels comfortable with— if he just wants to look briefly, then play with a toy, fine.

If he wants to stroke the baby's hands or feet (gently), or even sit with the baby on his lap with you supporting the baby's head, fine. Let him set the pace.

helping out

2-5 years

Let your child help you with the baby. It's important that she feels a part of the process (although also bear in mind that some kids will want no part of it—so don't force). Washing the baby's tummy at bathtime, running for a diaper, finding the baby's new toy—all of these simple actions are helpful. Don't be surprised, in fact, if she wants to take over care of the baby entirely and in a few weeks is giving you instructions on how to "do it right."

the new baby
2-5 years **when breastfeeding**

If you're breastfeeding your new baby, your toddler might be jealous of this close physical contact. Invite the firstborn to sit next to you. Let her rub the baby's leg while you read her a story—or if that's a bit too much juggling, just let her put on her favorite TV show and really watch it with her. Ask her questions about it and generally make her feel just as important as the baby in your arms.

baby milk

2-5 years

Some children start to want to nurse again and might even ask for the option. I actually expressed a bit of milk into a cup for one of my children who wanted to try it. He sipped it and immediately asked for juice—he also never asked to nurse again! If you are uncomfortable doing this, or it doesn't work, simply make it clear that the milk inside mommy's breasts is just for babies. Let him know that he had it once and then he got bigger and got to drink lots of different things. Make sure he understands that the baby won't be nursing forever, and that he is too big to do it anymore.

balancing out

Make time for your older child. Sometimes you are going to
have to resist the temptation to clean or do laundry and
make good on that promise to take your firstborn to the
playground instead. Many experts say to make time for
each child alone, but frankly, as the mother of four with
parents out of state, I found that absolutely impossible. I
always had to bring at least one or two along. Your child
has a little brother or sister now who is going to be around
forever, and he's going to have to get used to traveling as a
team. But make sure that you bring baby along to the older
child's activities at least as often as you drag your kid to
the baby's doctor appointments!

introduce other playmates

2-5 years

Ensure that your child is comfortable with other people in their life who can give special attention. No one could get near my firstborn without his screaming bloody murder. It took a week in 100 degree temperatures at the beach with my parents and sisters, while I was nine months pregnant and could hardly move, for my son to realize that all of these people were there to play with him. It made the arrival of the new baby much easier, because if mom was busy, he would go find grandma!

the new baby

2–5 years

toys for all

Visitors have to understand that big brothers and sisters need some attention, too. It hadn't occurred to me, but one of my good friends knew better than I and brought presents for my toddler son as well as my newborn daughter when she came to visit me in the hospital. My son immediately felt like a king and was proud to show off his baby sister—along with his brand new truck.

hold and sing

2–5 years

Have your toddler help you teach the baby songs and games (like patty-cake) that she knows by heart. Make sure your child has the chance to hold the baby sometimes while she does this—well supported by a pillow under her arms and the baby across her lap. Holding the baby and singing to her can help a toddler or preschooler really bond with the new life-form in her space. My little ones used to love to present the baby with different toys and do a show-and-tell type of thing where they would tell the baby what the toy was, let her touch it for a second, and then tell her things like, "When you get to be my age, you can play with this." Just make sure all such activities are supervised!

friends
and feuds

It seems like such a good idea...at first. You and another parent meet at a library story hour and bring your little ones for a play date. "This will be great," you think. "I'll get to talk to an actual grown-up, and my child will have someone to play with." But then, as the minutes together tick past, reality sets in. There is a fine line in a toddler's or preschooler's mind between being friends, being jealous, and being tired and cranky. They don't know why they are acting this way, just that they want what they want....There is hitting, snatching toys away, possibly even a bite or two, and someone ends up crying. "After laughing comes crying," my husband used to shout up the stairs to the children, and it's true. But there are some ways to prevent the jealousy and anger between friends before it occurs, and ways to calm it down afterward.

good intentions

2-5 years

Although jealousy can bubble up in children at the oddest moments, don't assume it is at the heart of every fight that breaks out. Consider each encounter individually and assume that the offending child's intentions were good. Let's say your child is playing nicely on the floor and your friend's child toddles over and grabs a toy from him. Instead of assuming jealousy over the toy, let's assume they just want to join in the fun. Adopting this perspective will help you and other moms be more patient.

21

friends and feuds
role play

Because it is often easier for children to share the sorrows
and misfortunes of classmates than to celebrate their
successes, children should be taught about jealousy and
how to handle it when such situations arise. One method
is to have children practice responses to others' joys and
accomplishments through role-play. For example, "Your
birthday was last month, and you asked for a puppy but
didn't get one. You find out the parents of your best friend
just gave her a puppy for her birthday, and your friend is
very happy. What do you say to her?" Understanding that
feelings of jealousy can cloud one's ability to help others
celebrate is the first step to surviving these situations.

keep playtime short 2-3 years

Up to an hour is enough for almost any child to the age of three. This is about the limit that most children have for sharing their toys with other children before they become tired, cranky, and as a result, jealous. As your child gets older and more used to playing with other children, the crankiness and resulting jealousy will remain at bay for longer periods.

friends and feuds

keep a date

Schedule most play dates either before your child's naptime or after, depending on which works best for you. Most kids go full blast when friends are over and wear themselves out more quickly than if they were alone. If your child has a regular 2 P.M. nap schedule—then schedule a lunch play date. The fun of having lunch with a friend coupled with a good run around outside, your child will be ready to nap in no time. Or, try putting them down for a nap before a play date—a well-rested child can be more resilient therefore less likely to succumb to a jealous tirade at the expense of your friend's child (or to rise to the bait!).

friends and feuds
keep a close eye
2–5 years

You can usually tell when a child is about to cause a bit of trouble. Watch your child when she's playing, and you'll see the gleam in her eye before she goes for the car in her buddy's hand. If you can step in with a positive redirection (presenting a similar car, for example) you can prevent a lot of stress and hurt feelings.

friends and feuds

neutral
territory

2-5 years

Sometimes it is just too hard for toddlers to share their own toys in their own room. So occasionally, I suggest to the other mom that we meet in a park or children's museum. Here the kids will be on an equal footing and this way, they can simply enjoy being together without being told by the adults to share their favorite toys.

be regular

Make the play dates regular. Doing this will help your child get used to the schedule, and also to the children he is playing with, thereby reducing the likelihood of jealousy and anger. Rather than scattering, try to schedule play dates as regularly as you can. As the children become close, you will notice that on, say, Tuesday, your child will remember that Sarah likes to play house while Kyle likes to play space rangers, and he will prepare himself accordingly.

2-5 years **remove her**

Often it is enough to remove your toddler from the setting for ten or 15 minutes so she can regain control. If she continues to balk, encourage her to express whatever emotion she's feeling by saying the words for her, such as, "You look angry." When your child has calmed down, say, "You're calm now, so we can go back to the other children." If she is so keyed up and going home is the best option, say your good-byes immediately. Don't make your child feel guilty for leaving, though. Remember that this is hard for her, too. She needs to know that you're her ally in helping her learn and benefit from self-control.

don't overplan the play 2-5 years

Kids who are shuttled from one fun "project" to the next, without getting the chance to just play, get angry and frustrated sooner, creating more potential for jealous behavior—like yanking toys out of each other's hands. When children are in a room together with a supervising grown-up and a pile of toys, the fun is there waiting.

friends and feuds

sit back

The point of a play group is to allow parents to relax, too. So, sit back and let your children enjoy each other. Be vigilant without being involved. One of the best skills I learned over the years was how to sit and drink my coffee and still spot an accident waiting to happen. The key to neutralizing danger is to walk quietly over to the offending child, who perhaps is swinging a plastic golf club over your child's head, disable said child with a cheerful, "Let's keep that on the ground," and return to your seat. If it wasn't your child, the mother will probably thank you for being so cool, and you will have prevented both the crying from the child about to be hit and the screaming from the child about to be punished for hitting the other child.

friends and feuds
discuss the "rules" 2-5 years

Parents need to determine how they are going to handle sticky situations between kids before the they occur. If you are in favor of disciplining each other's children, decide in what way. Agree on a time-out place and bear in mind that some parents, even when they say it's okay, get offended when someone else scolds their child. If another parent is not disciplining her child, then the best thing to do is to remove your own child from harm's way.

siblings
close in age

Ah...brothers and sisters. My first two were born only 14 months apart and I was often asked, "Are they twins?" (leading me to want to respond, "Yes, we just don't feed one...") I have heard more horror stories about sibling rivalry than almost any other issue except potty training. There seem to be two camps on the issue: those who have their children close together; and those who have them far apart. Well, three camps, since there are those who avoid the problem altogether by only having one child! But, if you have decided, as I have more than once, that your family will not be complete without the addition of someone else, then you will have to face some sibling battles. Here are some tips if you are in the first camp and have children close together in age.

different treats

All children are not created equally—and should not be treated as such. This is a tough one because it is so tempting just to buy two of everything. In the long term, though, it is not always practical. "How come Lydia got new shoes and I didn't?" I'll hear. You have to make it clear that: a.) the shoes currently on the offended child's feet were new last month; and b.) just because one child gets something it doesn't mean the other has to get something, too.

33

close in age

who's the favorite

This was an easy question to answer when I just had two children—of different sexes no less—because I could answer, "Lydia is my favorite little girl in the whole wide world, and Matthew is my favorite little boy." As more brothers were added to the family roll call, I had to start defining favorites by age: "You're my favorite four-year-old in the whole wide world." This makes each child feel special and like the favorite without actually being the favorite. You can also define certain things that you like the most about a child...without denigrating another child. Children don't really care if they're the favorite—most, I expect, know that

their parents love all of them equally—they just want to

feel that they stand out

in some special way and

that their parents

recognize this, too.

close in age

minimize comparisons

This is especially important as children get older. My first two, now in school, are constantly comparing grades. It drives me buggy because the older one will say, "I got all As in math," and I have to reemphasize that the younger of the two is in a different math class, with a different teacher. It's important to remember that each child has her own

particular skills, aptitudes, and interests. You shouldn't judge one against the other—and neither should they. Saying things like, "Why can't you get better grades like your brother," is only going to make your child feel worse about her performance and will inspire nothing more than her trying to trip her older brother when you're not looking.

close in age

hear both sides
of the story

2 years and up

The only sound I hate more than an unhappy, crying child is
the sound of two sets of feet stomping down the stairs as
each child prepares to tell me what the other has done.
I take a deep breath and then call on them one at a time to
explain the issue. Sometimes, I refuse to get involved,
particularly if it's about something silly like a television
show. That one is easily solved with a "Turn off the TV and
go clean your rooms." I usually won't hear about it again.
On the other hand, if the children are starting to abuse
each other, hitting or calling names, then you must
intervene. My best punishment ever? "You are not allowed

to play with each other for the rest of the day." I wouldn't let them talk to one another or do anything together. They wouldn't admit to it, but they missed each other and were visibly pleased when I allowed them to play together again.

close in age

odd and even days

This works particularly well with young children and can hold steady through the teenage years. During one family vacation, my father actually implemented this strategy for my two younger sisters, then about nine and 11 years old. One sister had a birthday on an odd day, the other on an even day. From then on, the person whose "day" it was, was allowed to pick the TV show, the playground location,

whatever. Whenever a decision was required, the person of the day got to make it. I added a bit of a twist, however, when I implemented this system for my own children. They got into a habit of envying the person whose "day" it was, so in addition to being able to pick the fun stuff, that person also had to do the worst chore of the day—usually the dinner dishes.

close in age

humor heals
most wounds

2 years and up

Siblings who are close in age often just get sick of one another, especially if the weather has been bad and they've been cooped up together for a while. This can lead to all kinds of jealousy issues, like, "You always let her do what she wants" or "Why does Matt get to play with the Nintendo first?" One time, the bickering and wrestling had gotten to a point where I couldn't take it any more, so I told my two oldest to go and fight it out, outside in the rain. They looked at me like I was crazy but dutifully went outside, in the rain, and ended up running around, laughing and splashing each other. They came inside drenched and muddy, but they had stopped fighting, and while one made hot chocolate for the both of them, the other got out a board game—shocking!

interests apart
close in age

2 years and up

They don't have to be together all of the time. Try to develop your children's various interests and promote their individuality. It's difficult, particularly when they are very young but try to do separate things with each child— maybe bake a cake with one child for a special dinner, and with the other draw pictures to use as placemats. In time, you will notice each child's own interests and can promote them accordingly.

close in age
2 years and up **teamwork**

While it is important to let them do separate things, at the same time, make sure they also know how to work together. If they are in a spurt of active dislike of each other, have them clean a room together or rake leaves. It is essential that siblings know they are in this for life, and promoting teamwork will, hopefully, keep your family close as the children grow up and leave home.

close in age
family time

2 years and up

Do things together as a family. It is easy to get into a habit of always letting your children do separate activities—one's at a friend's house, another's at soccer—but we have found that some of our best family moments, reinforcing sibling relationships, take place on camping trips or even just at home. On someone's birthday, for example, we have a special family ritual—we all take turns telling each other what our favorite thing about the birthday boy or girl is. And they can't just say things like, "I like his CD collection." I make them dig deep, which involves some fun strolls down memory lane.

close in age

ignore the small stuff

2 years and up

Despite what some experts say, it is not all small stuff. But arguments over toys, games, TV, or dinner are not accepted in my house. If they start over a toy, I let them know in no uncertain terms that they can either work it out or I am taking the toy and throwing it away. "You have one minute to decide," I say, and then I walk away. More often than not, the toy is set aside and a new game is begun. However, in those instances when they continue to fight about it, I take the toy and "throw it away" (usually I put it on the shelf in my bedroom closet—particularly if it is an expensive toy!). Children need to know that you mean business and that you won't waver just because you want your peace and quiet. The look on their faces when you take that disputed toy is usually punishment enough for them—and frankly, a bit humorous for you!

look out for the big stuff

You have to be aware of how your children are treating each other. I allow a normal amount of rivalry in the house. I know they are not always going to agree or be nice to each other, but when they start calling each other nasty names or putting each other down, I won't listen to it. If one child is verbally abusive to another, you have to put your foot down. I'll often pull the children aside and ask the offender if anyone ever speaks like that to them.

Be careful, because this can quickly escalate into a "he said, she said" argument. If so, I'll ask specifically if I ever say things like that to them. When they respond "no," I'll have them explain to me why not. I'll also have the offending child explain how they feel when someone calls them names. This works very well for younger children, but as they get older, however, the flip responses become more frequent and you sometimes have to take a harsher stance (grounding, taking away privileges, etc.).

siblings with a
large age gap

Being the older with much younger sibs can be either a blessing or a burden. It is often said that waiting at least four years between children will prevent, to some extent, sibling rivalry. After all, the thinking goes, the older child will be able to understand about a new baby. However, speaking not as a mom but as the oldest in a family with sisters seven and nine years younger, I can tell you unequivocally that sibling rivalry occurs even between children with a large age gap, and in some instances the jealousy on both sides can be even more intense. So, here are some tips that originate from both perspectives—a parent's and an oldest sibling's .

the comforter

4 years and up

Promote the older sibling's abilities to comfort the younger child. My ten-year-old daughter is brilliant at reacting quickly to my five-year-old when he falls or otherwise hurts himself outside. She is right on the scene and sometimes will even carry him into the house so I can examine the injury. She is also there for emotional support when I clean that freshly scraped knee and is great at going and getting a Band-Aid and other items. While I do the "mean" job of cleaning up, she holds his hand and tells him that "it isn't so bad."

large age gap

the supervisor

Let the older child have some supervisory duties over the younger child. This could include letting a four- or five-year-old "watch" the baby (who is strapped safely in an infant seat) while you do something quick like going to the bathroom or answering the phone. It doesn't have to be a long separation, and the confidence and trust you instill in your oldest will be well worth any worry you experience. When they were older, my third child—no longer the one being looked after, loved showing his younger brother the "right" way to climb the jungle gym.

large age gap
the teacher
4 years and up

Older children enjoy teaching the younger ones a skill. Whether it's helping them write their letters or numbers, or teaching them to play board games, it is really magical when you observe one child teaching another. I will never forget the day when I walked in on my then nine-year-old son teaching his five-year-old brother how to play chess! I felt like I had two little geniuses under my roof—of course, they later fought over who got to play with the computer, but whatever!

large age gap

put them in the same room

This is one that has to be determined by age and by the nature of your older child, but letting the children share a room (once the baby has begun sleeping through the night) will help keep your children close. I found that my oldest would sometimes get up with the youngest on a Saturday morning and make him breakfast before I even knew they were awake!

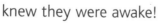

54

large age gap

give them separate rooms

4 years and up

If your oldest is much older—I'd say six or seven years older at least—it may be better to keep them in separate rooms (if space allows). Children already of school age can resent having a younger sibling in their space. This is particularly true as older children develop an interest in more complex toys, like small Legos, or collections. This can not only be dangerous for the younger child because of potential choking hazards, but it can also really make an older child angry when he gets home to discover that the model airplane he worked on for weeks has been transformed into a pile of rubble in the hands of the little one. If it is impossible to give your children separate rooms, give the older child a special and secure space to keep his more valuable possessions—a high shelf or a closet you can latch.

large age gap

co-sleeping

Our youngest child, be it the first or fourth, always found a home in our bed. But as they began to sleep in their own beds, they sometimes found comfort sleeping with another sibling. My oldest son will occasionally "camp out" and sleep next to my youngest if he is having nightmares, and my youngest has been known to crawl into bed with his older sister in the middle of the night. As much as they would hate to admit it, I think this illustrates the deep affection they have for one another. On the other hand, if it becomes too much of a habit for the younger one, he can become a pest. We have found in our family, however, that this is only an occasional occurrence. Their willingness to sleep together is also helpful when we are traveling, because often the children have to share beds in a hotel or guest room. In the company of his older siblings, the youngest is not frightened of being separated from us, and the older children enjoy the feeling of responsibility.

patience with all ages

It's a common scenario: the older one has just gotten out a game and left for a minute to go to the bathroom or get a snack—and when she comes back, she finds that the baby or toddler has overturned the game, scattering the pieces everywhere, so now she's coming after you to make things right. What do you do? Of course, you explain that it was unintentional and that the younger one is "only a baby," but what if the oldest one is tired of that excuse? Well, first, don't get angry with the older child for not understanding. Listen to her concerns and then help her set the game back up, this time in a quiet room or on the kitchen table—somewhere out of reach of the little one.

If you make an effort to understand your older child's pain, it will go a long way toward limiting her resentment of the younger one.

large age gap

bossiness

As much as I adore my daughter for being helpful with her younger brothers, sometimes she can be a bit too helpful! Keep an ear out for the times when helpful guidance turns bossy and sometimes a bit degrading to the younger child. Your oldest might think she is just helping, but she also has to understand that a younger child can do things for himself sometimes and that you are still the mother. I knew things with my daughter were getting a little out of hand when she interrupted me during a conversation with my two youngest boys, telling me who had really thrown the ball at the cat—I think she was even ready to dole out punishments! I told her that I appreciated all the help, but that when I needed her, I would let her know.

large age gap

keep special toys separate

4 years and up

Hand-me-downs are a great benefit of having more than one child, but don't be too quick to hand everything down. Your older child will certainly have some opinions on which toys your youngest child is "allowed" to have. Consult your child when taking things from his space and you'll find that he will start bringing you all kinds of things you had forgotten about to "give to the baby."

large age gap

treasure chest

Be prepared to hold some things back, too. You might find your daughter is very attached to a certain dress or stuffed animal. Let her keep that dress—even if it's too small.

Perhaps set up a little treasure chest of her own where she can put photos, old clothes she likes, and other special items. Just be sure it doesn't get to the point where she's hording everything— firmer guidance might be needed then!

hold regular family meetings

large age gap

4 years and up

These can take place at the dinner table or even in the car. Once a month—or once a week—gather everyone together and air grievances. Anything goes in these meetings at our house, from the petty to the major. Just make a few ground rules, in order to keep children from insulting or ganging up on one another. This is a great time, too, for children to voice complaints against their parents without fear of punishment! It also allows me to let each of them know how I think they're doing with their chores, grades, whatever. Be sure to end each meeting on a positive note, with everyone saying what they like most about each person in the family or planning a family treat.

pets and kids

Whether you have a pet and are bringing a new baby home to it, or you have children and are considering a new pet, there are many things to consider beforehand. I will assume that you have already researched breeds (of pets, that is) and are confident that your current pet or the one you are purchasing is family-friendly. If you are uncertain of this, a local veterinarian should be able to help. Pets and children can be a wonderful mix, and the love between a child and his dog or cat can be a delight. However, just as children can be jealous, so can dogs or even cats. These tips should help you make the process of adding a new member to the family an easier and more enjoyable one for both your two-footed and four-footed children.

pet planning

Animals, particularly dogs and cats, are creatures of habit, and the arrival of a new baby, be it your first or third, can throw them for a loop. If you must change the routine of your current pet, for example allocating a new feeding location or restricting entry to a room or two, do so before the new arrival. If a different walk time will be implemented, adjust that beforehand as well.

pets and kids
set boundaries

Set boundaries for acceptable interactions between the dog
and your child. If the child or dog doesn't respect these,
take away privileges. If they do, offer positive reinforcement.
Let them stay up past their bedtime or have a special treat
like ice cream. And don't forget to treat your dog. He could
get a special biscuit, which shows him he has done well.

Grurrr

supervise, supervise, supervise!

I can't say this enough. Introduce your pet to your baby slowly and for only short periods of time. Be aware of any adverse behavior, including baring of teeth, hair sticking up on the dog's neck, or even low growls. Don't leave them alone together, even if you are positive you have the sweetest dog—or cat—in the world. To your pet, you are the "alpha" male or female, and he responds to you appropriately because he knows you are in charge. A new,

little baby could be, to some pets, a creature to break into the hierarchy of your household— and animals usually fight those battles out.

pets and kids
wait a while

Do not get a new, young pet at the same time as you bring home a new baby. You may think it will be great to let your baby and puppy grow up together, but actually, it's a terrible idea. Both require too much time and attention, and the new puppy or kitten will almost certainly get ignored when time is limited. Hold off until you are confident in yourself as a new parent and have sufficient time to devote to the pet.

pets and kids

teach your children

Children who are jealous of a pet sometimes play too aggressively with it. Teach your children how to play with animals. Poking, riding, kicking—even in a playful way—can look like an attack to a dog and provoke "attack games." Lead by example, showing your child how to play with the dog, feed it, and groom it, allowing your child to participate in both the chores and joys of the pet. Even very young children can fill a dog's bowl with food or brush its hair.

pets and kids
don't exclude your pet

Be sure to include your pet in your daily life. If you are constantly scolding him and telling him to get down or not get near that (whether it's a baby toy or the infant seat), he will soon begin to feel jealous and neglected. This is when many problems begin. When you come home with your new baby, or any time you return home with the kids for that matter, greet your pet cheerfully and let him know he has been missed. Call him and pet him when you're done changing a diaper. Even talking to him while you're feeding the baby can make him feel included.

pets and kids
training sessions

Lisa Rosenthal, author of *A Dog's Best Friend*, explains that
children may exhibit jealousy toward the family pet by
being aggressive. To avoid this, enroll your family in dog
training sessions. Bring your youngest kids along so they
can learn and participate, too. You'll find that the instructor
will reinforce the message you've been giving your kids—
that puppies need respect and care—not antagonizing.

toy tactics

Some animals, particularly dogs, get very attached to their toy. If your child is playing a fetch game with a dog and the dog refuses to give up the ball or stick, make sure your child understands it is important not to force the dog. A tug-of-war will ensue and if the dog gets angry, worse can happen. If a child is having trouble, tell him to ask an adult for help, or better yet, just let the dog bring him the toy on his own. He will if he really wants to.

pets and kids
safe zone

If you have a crate for your puppy, Lisa Rosenthal says, teach your kids that this is your dog's "safe zone." Explain that just as they sometimes want to be left alone, the puppy needs his own space, too. Teach your children that this is a safe zone for your puppy where he can go to be alone. If you don't have a crate, then it would be a worthwhile investment.

pets and kids
on the same level

Your dog is bound to be jealous as he watches you pay a lot of attention to the new creature in the house. Spend some time with your baby on your lap while sitting on the floor. Don't pressure your dog to come to you, Rosenthal says, but call him and see if he'd like a pet. Your dog is curious

about this new being who is getting so much of your attention. Never force your dog to be close to your baby, but spend time down on his level. This will feed his curiosity and help him to understand that this new member of the family is important but is not there to replace him.

sense of smell

Apply baby lotion or powder to your hands—or whatever scented products you might use, including diaper cream—and allow your pet to smell them before the baby comes. Letting him sniff new blankets, clothes, and diapers will also benefit him. Start placing things, like diapers or toys, where they will be when the new baby comes—this includes on the dining room table or couch where things will likely end up!

That way, your pet can smell that new baby smell around the house and it will become a part of the atmosphere. You can also begin to train him to leave those things alone if he has a knack for taking things! For reasons of hygiene, baby toys and dog toys should remain separate, so you may have to be extra vigilant, at least at first, about not leaving baby's things around the house.

problems with
parents

I know it's difficult to imagine, but there are times when a parent, under certain conditions, can succumb to the green-eyed monster, too. Most often this occurs when one half of a couple tries to get back into the swing of things romantically. It is difficult sometimes either for the father to start to view mom as a sexy being again, making mom a little jealous of her former self, or for dad to feel special again because mom is spending so much time with baby. Couples who were romantically fine after one baby might find the addition of two or three little ones even harder to overcome. These tips should help you and your partner reconnect and get over any jealousy and hurt feelings after the baby is born.

fathers need a role

Men often see women as the primary childcare giver and so participate only passively with their baby, which could lead to their feeling left out and even jealous. Men are often conditioned to hold back their feelings—especially softer ones, such as hurt. So when they feel excluded, they withdraw, rather than try to get involved. It is important that fathers get in the mix by seeking a role and learning parenting skills.

problems with parents
accept the strain

Having a baby will throw you and your partner for a loop for quite some time. Between the sleep deprivation, economic pressures, the barrage of advice you are receiving, the new parenting skills you have to learn, and possibly the pain that you are in after giving birth, the joy of having a baby can quickly dissolve into panic and frustration. A partner who is counting the six weeks until you can have sex again will only add to the pressure! Both partners need to accept outright that things will be abnormal for a while until you discover a new "normal." This will go a long way toward keeping you close, rather than jealous or possessive.

take care of yourself

You are entering a period when your energy will shift from keeping yourself together to keeping another human being together. You will be amazed at how much time and focus it takes just to get through the day with an infant. Some days you feel lucky to get your hair brushed. It is important during this time to plan in little breaks for yourself. Maybe a friend or relative could stay with the baby while you take a 15-minute walk, or a 20-minute bath, or have an hour date with your partner.

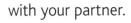

go to bed before you're tired

Remember how in the old days you used to be able to stay awake as late as you wanted to? Parents with kids living in their home never have enough time—they stay in the laundry room or on the computer until they are seeing double. Then they tumble into bed exhausted, wearing whatever they put on to cook dinner. This is a romantic "don't" so if you want to feel close to your partner, make sure you go to bed well before you are ready to collapse on the floor.

have a giggle

Spend a few minutes giggling and joking about together. I don't know about you, but humor, even more than lust, is the tie that binds in my marriage. Sharing a laugh together in bed is worth ten minutes of foreplay. Well, ten minutes of light foreplay anyway.

problems with parents
start at the beginning

Start the seduction at the front door. Yeah, I know your sleeves are wet up to the elbows from baby bathwater and your hair looks like Marge Simpson's, but pausing for a real sweet kiss during that evening reunion pays dividends later in the evening.

time it right

Don't talk about sex over dinner. In fact, don't discuss intimacy of any sort during the hellish hours between dinner, the kids' baths, and their bedtime. It always sounds like a bad idea when you're looking at a sink full of dirty dishes. Wait at least 30 minutes after the last child has retired and you've had half a glass of wine. I promise, it will sound a lot more appealing then.

problems with parents
make the first move

Men quickly learn that there are several other people and concerns that can take precedence over their needs. After a while, they stop bothering to make overtures, since they know that a toddler with a fever or a little daughter not getting invited to a class birthday party trumps them every time. It's our job as mother-of-all, babe of one, to reassure our beloved that we are interested and can still focus on him.

problems with parents
come clean

This is particularly important for the men in the room. If this is your first baby, no doubt your wife is feeling more than a bit overwhelmed. You may not want to contribute to her problems by unloading yours on her, but do it. Be as clear and simple about it as possible, without sounding like you're expecting too much. If you want more private time with your wife, don't just say that, but come to the table with a solution—like asking a grandparent to babysit for a few hours. This will show your wife that you care about both of you, not just your own needs.

delegate

The secret of enjoying larger families (although it is beneficial for smaller ones as well) is to delegate. As your children reach appropriate ages, it is possible to obtain their "help," increasing their sense of worth and giving you a break. Develop a strategy for dividing daily chores in a routine manner with the children enlisted to help. Washing dishes, putting toys away at a specific time of day, and encouraging children to play "on their own" for 20 minutes while you and Dad have "talking time" can become their "jobs" in the family. Age-appropriate duties encourage children to become responsible adults, and some form of "helping" can start as early as two years of age.

connect with other moms

Develop friendships and activities outside your partner and baby that can recharge your batteries. Consider joining a mothers' group and sharing your feelings with other women. Often we feel jealous, but we aren't exactly sure what we are jealous of—women without babies? Dad's ability to get up and go right after the baby is born? The baby? Connecting with other moms, all of whom have been there, is a great way to get these feelings out and often to laugh about them.

sharing with
each other

Ah yes, your precious little one is walking and talking and one of the words your angel has just forcibly used, in a manner rivaling that of Linda Blair in *The Exorcist*, is "MINE!". Most children, at one time or another, hate to share—whether it's with their sibling or with their best friend. Sharing is a tough topic because while we want our children to "play nice," it often requires restraint that little ones not only don't have, but they don't want to have either. So, how do you get your child to understand the value behind giving his toys away to other children— even if it's only for an afternoon?

show them,
don't tell them

It's quite easy, in a child's eyes, for mom to tell him to let
another child play with his toy when she doesn't have to let
the friend's mom drive her car or eat her cookie. So, with
another mom or an older child,
demonstrate sharing. "I'm giving
the toy to Annabel and in ten
minutes she will give the toy
back to me,"
and then make
sure she does!

sharing with each other
2–5 years **play together**

If children are fighting over the same toy, show them how they can enjoy the toy together, by rolling a ball or a truck between them, for example. Games like this rarely last very long and soon enough one of the children will walk off to find entertainment elsewhere.

sharing with each other
ask the question
3-5 years

Children between the ages of three and five should be able to work a conflict out between them. When children come screaming at me about a certain toy, I always ask first if anyone is hurt and then simply announce that this is not for me to decide. "It looks like you both love that toy, so how do you think you can play with it together?" They will usually come up with a plan, either simple or very elaborate, for playing with the toy.

sharing with each other

double up

If possible, arrange to have two similar toys—particularly a popular one—around during the play time. If the hammer and pegs toy was the hit (forgive the pun) at the last play date, perhaps the friend's mom could bring his set over, too. At the beginning of summer, I always buy one of those baskets full of cheap sand toys to take to the beach or the pool, and that way, when other children try to take my child's shovel away, I can give them an extra. I write our last name in permanent marker on the bottom in the hope of getting all of the toys back, but I don't sweat it if a bucket is missing at the end of the day!

sharing with each other
one pile for each
2-4 years

If the children are very young, separate the toys (at least initially) into two piles. You can avoid a lot of arguments and hurt feelings this way and will probably find that the children start to barter their toys or begin to share them on their own. This gives each child a sense of ownership over his pile and allows them to "parallel play," something children under three often do—together, but separately.

sharing with each other

2-5 years   **put away favorites**

Allow your child to take three or four favorite toys—ones
he is particularly protective over—and place them in a
closet where no one can get to them. Explain to your child
that doing this means that all of his other toys are fair
game for the other children to play with, but that these
special ones will be safe while his friends are over. Also
remind your child that if he puts these toys away so they
can't be shared, then he can't play with them in front of
the other children either. This may even inspire your child
to share the prized toys.

be specific in your instructions

2–5 years

Children are very literal, as we well know, and will exploit every opportunity to take advantage of this ("But mom, you didn't say I couldn't climb the bookshelf and jump to the couch..."). So, make it perfectly clear that grabbing toys from other children will not be allowed and that everyone is allowed a turn on the slide. Just saying, "Play nice," leaves you too open for, "I was nice when I blocked him from getting on the swing."

sharing with each other
2-5 years **power of one**

Help your child recognize the power of his actions. Your child snatches an action figure from his playmate's hand and now the playmate is crying. Instead of scolding, go to your child and say, "How would you feel if I took this toy away from you right now?"—and then do it. Your child will be shocked that you took the toy away and will be better able to put his own action in perspective.

sharing with each other
give it back

2-5 years

Too often parents just yell, "Give it back," to the offending child and when it doesn't happen, shrug their shoulders and put it down to toddlerhood. Don't accept this. Take your child by the hand and bring her and her toy over to the child she took it from. Have her apologize and give the toy back and then have a time out (if you feel the message was not completely received) away from her friends.

sharing with each other

praise voluntary sharing

Sometimes, a child will shock the heck out of you and offer a toy without being asked. When your child shares voluntarily, make sure you acknowledge her generosity and praise it, not just accepting that it's how she should have acted in the first place. Reinforcing good behavior will motivate your child to get your attention with positive actions rather than with negative moves.

sharing with each other
sometimes, you don't have to share

2-5 years

It's important for a child to know that his mom or dad is on his side when sharing is not necessary. Let's say your child just got a new bike, and you have taken him to the park. A child you have never seen before comes up and asks to take a ride on the bike (this will happen eventually, I promise, with bikes, sand toys, etc). Do you have to make your child share the bike in an effort to reinforce the benefits of sharing? Of course not. You can show your child in this instance how to say a polite "No" or "Maybe next time," and ride away. Back your child up and let him know that sometimes we don't have to share, particularly if it's someone we don't know.

school days

Sending your child off to school or day care can introduce new jealousy issues. Children often feel envious of other children's clothes, toys, friends, or houses when they begin school. There is no easy way to deal with this except to keep it in perspective and know that children often act in phases—sometimes they will be absolutely confident in their own uniqueness, other times they will want to do everything everyone else is doing. And while these tips generally apply to the child under eight, they can be helpful in one form or another through the pre-teen years!

clothing wars

Even children under the age of eight can be jealous of other kids' clothes. Find out just what it is about another child's clothes that your child especially likes. It could be simply that they're new rather than your child's hand-me-downs, or a special cartoon character T-shirt. If the latter is out of your budget or out of your accepted style, see if you can reach a compromise. Just adding one or two items to a child's wardrobe is better than buying all new clothes.

school days
3-8 years
more clothing wars

Sometimes the clothing war stems from your child's friend wearing items displaying images from a cartoon or movie that you have deemed unacceptable for your own child. This occurs frequently in my home because I won't allow my children to watch popular shows like *Teenage Mutant Ninja Turtles* and, more recently, *Pokemon*. Be firm in your resolve to keep such items out of the house. Explain your reasoning to your child (mine is that such shows portrayed violence in too flattering a light). Then, offer alternatives, such as buying a T-shirt or backpack from a character line your child likes and is allowed to watch.

explain the budget

If money is the reason you won't buy those $40-and-up sneakers or name-brand jeans, then have your child shop with you. Even children around the age of four or five understand that if $100 is your back-to-school shopping budget, then spending $40 of it on sneakers leaves very little to be spent on other items. Have your child keep a running total on a calculator (with your help, of course). She will soon see that she gets a lot more by spending $10 a piece on new clothes instead of $20 or $30.

school days
3–8 years **speaking out**

Some children are jealous of another child's ability to make friends easily or speak out in class. If this is the case with your child, encourage him to speak out at home and present his news with confidence. Learning this skill early on will help your child to make new friends and participate in classroom activities.

make them feel worthy 3-8 years

Putting children down at home can lead to many problems at school. I know, I know, you would never put your child down. But sometimes we do it, even if it's only unconsciously. Children who feel they are not worth much at home will feel like they are worth even less in a strange atmosphere and will not offer their opinions willingly.

3–8 years **teacher favoritism**

Sometimes a teacher will play favorites at school, or at least our children think they do. Maybe your child comes home and complains that the teacher calls on everyone else but her or that other students are always at the front of the line and she never gets a chance. Before you change classes, talk with the teacher. You may find that your child is the type who always raises her hand and the teacher is just trying to give other students a chance.

away from the group   3-8 years

Kids can get jealous for what appear to be the craziest reasons. Perhaps your child has been shunned by kids at school or daycare just because one kid didn't like his sneakers (I know, it's silly, but...). Invite just one child over at a time, not as a group or for a party, so that your child will have the chance to get to know each kid individually. That way, they can all see just how cool your child really is and he can bond with them in more relaxed conditions. It's amazing how well children get along with one another when they are outside the group atmosphere of school.

School days
3-8 years **comfort in a friend**

Even at very young ages children can form cliques.
Sometimes, groups of children will get together and shun
another child for what appears to be no reason at all. Your
child may be jealous of the clique, while the kids in the
group could be envious of your child's good grades or
whatever. Children who have trouble making friends can
become angry and even more jealous. Encourage your child
to try to make just one good friend and not worry about
being in a group. A good friend can be a comfort during a
long school day, and if that friend has other friends, she
can introduce your child to a new "crowd."

be an example

This is true in almost everything about parenting. If you are very conscious of what the neighbors are driving or doing in their yard, or if you will only buy a certain brand of peanut butter, it is only natural that your child will become very picky about what he wants, perhaps becoming a little too influenced by the trends in school.

If you can, make a family decision to deemphasize the importance of brands and labels in your world, and your children will tend to care less about them as well.

NON
BR

BRAND

school days
teach appreciation

It's a hard thing to teach, I know, but I found that if I was always going on about the new car that so-and-so had or the fact that my much younger sister (without four children to support) had much nicer clothes, I was, in essence permitting my children to be jealous of their peers. Showing appreciation for what we do have and demonstrating that to our children, can go a long way toward your child learning to appreciate his own stuff.

time alone

Often kids feel jealous because they are being excluded at school or at home. My daughter is the lone girl among three boys, for example, and there is only so much touch football she can take before she starts getting cranky...no one ever wants to play what she wants to play. So, I asked her aunts to take her to their house for a weekend or a night and have a "girls' day out." This has worked wonders. My sisters take her out for breakfast and shopping and she can vent about her brothers or whatever problems she is having in school. This makes her feel special so when she has a bad week with brothers or friends, she has a place to go where she feels like a queen!

working
moms

As a mom it seems that no matter what we choose, staying at home or working, we are bound to feel guilty, no matter how happy we are with our decision. Another feeling that wells up frequently in many of the moms I have talked with is jealousy. We might be envious of our stay-at-home counterparts, or jealous of our nanny's or day care provider's ability to spend so much time with our children. Many moms express jealous feelings when they feel their day care provider might be getting a little too close to their children, leaving them out of the loop. Don't worry, there are ways to deal with these emotions, start by reassuring yourself that your child will always prefer you over whomever is taking care of him during the day.

working moms
devise a nanny contract

This is a good way (and it's never too late to write one up) to clarify not only the rate of pay and days off, but the types of issues and policies you want your nanny to be aware of. The contract can cover everything from pacifier usage to types of food you want your child to avoid. It also goes a long way toward establishing the business relationship between you and your child's carer.

working moms
evaluate your feelings

You wouldn't be the first person to get a lump in your throat when you hear your child mistakenly call your nanny, "mom." It's painful, but don't get upset with your child—or nanny. It could be that your child is simply associating the word "mom" with caregiver. But if it's really bothering you, share you concerns with your nanny and ask her how she thinks your child is feeling. You might gain some useful insights into your child's—and your nanny's—emotional state.

working moms
don't fret

It's a good thing if your baby is happy to see your caregiver! I know, you'd like her to make a bit of a fuss when she leaves you, but if she goes off happily it most likely means that she knows you'll be back for her. A secure baby is a blessing. Don't feel guilty for working and doing what makes you happy. If you would be miserable at home, then your baby would know this. Isn't it better to meet up with her later on—feeling satisfied—than hang out with her all day, unhappy because you aren't doing what you'd like to do—or are worried about money? Just be sure to cuddle your baby and spend time doing even the most mundane tasks when you are with her so she knows you are all in this family together.

working moms
treat with respect

Speak in nonconfrontational tones. Treat your nanny as you prefer to have people treat you at work. Don't criticize her in front of others, and begin and end conversations on a positive note. This will go a long way toward creating a respectful relationship between the two of you, and hopefully the end result is better overall care for your child.

be receptive...

... to your nanny's suggestions. She is, after all, the one person who is constantly with your child. It might irk you, but she could be the one observing, for example, when your child is showing signs of potty-training readiness. Soliciting advice from your nanny also shows your respect for her—even if you choose not to take it. Just remember, ultimately, you are the parent and you make the final decisions regarding your child's welfare.

working moms
learn from the past

When interviewing new candidates for the nanny job, ask how they'd handle some of the situations that were points of contention with your last nanny. Screen their responses before you give away your personal views on child rearing. And feel confident in knowing that, in your children's eyes, you can never hire someone to replace you as their parent.

daily activities

Check in with your caregiver about your child's daily activities. This kind of ongoing knowledge keeps you abreast of your child's development and allows you to participate in his life and anticipate his needs. You can then make time for activities that deepen your involvement in his day-to-day life. Preparing cupcakes together for the birthday of your son's best friend, or purchasing a good-bye gift for one of your son's daycare buddies, who is moving out of town, is a chance to be a part of your child's experience, even when you are not physically present.

daytime interaction

If your child is school-aged, stay in touch with classroom activities and your child's teacher. If possible, make yourself available by phone for your child or the teacher during the day. Children feel very secure and special when they can call a parent at work—not just in an emergency, but to report on their day, or even to get the occasional homework help by phone. In the evening, check with your child about assignments and help him get organized for the next school day.

working moms

time off for important events

Occasionally, make a point of taking time off from work in order to attend an important function or activity that involves your child. Your son or daughter will delight in coming first in these instances, and you will both remember these special events.

working moms
sharing everyday

Establish daily routines that promote sharing, such as checking in with your child at dinnertime and tucking her in at bedtime. Save 15 to 25 minutes per day to relate one-on-one with your child. Even teenagers enjoy a back rub and will talk to you as they relax at the end of a long day. You may be surprised how calm you feel when you end your day connecting with your child.

create routines

This means knowing your child's schedule and telling him where you will be and what you are doing, too! Children feel connected to their parents when they know what their work is about: schedule a visit to the office and share interesting and appropriate work stories with your child. On the weekends, plan one-on-one activities and family outings. Movies, sports events, simple gardening, and other activities can strengthen family bonds.

further reading

FABER, ADELE AND MAZLISH, ELAINE.
*How to Talk So Kids Will Listen and
Listen So Kids Will Talk.*
MacMillan Publishing Company, 1980.

FABER, ADELE AND MAZLISH, ELAINE
(CONTRIBUTOR).
Siblings Without Rivalry.
W.W. Norton & Company, 1990.

IOVINE, VICKI.
*The Girlfriends' Guide to Surviving
the First Year of Motherhood.*
Perigee, 1997.

STEPHENS, HELEN.
Toddler Story Book: What About Me?
Dorling Kindersley Publishing, 1999.

WOLF, ANTHONY E.
*Mom, Jason's Breathing on Me:
The Solution to Sibling Bickering.*
Ballantine Books, 2003.

WOLF, ANTHONY E.
*"It's Not Fair, Jeremy Spencer's
Parents Let Him Stay Up All Night!": A
Guide to the Tougher Parts of Parenting.*
Noonday Press, 1996.

notes

Acknowledgments

I would like to thank my children, my husband, John
Hogan, my mother, Rebecca Saraceno, and Mandy
Greenfield for all of their help and encouragement.

index